Dover Castle

Steven Brindle

Introduction

Dover Castle is one of the great landmarks and symbols of England, its towers and curtain walls greeting overseas visitors and returning Britons alike as the ferries sail into the harbour below. It guards the Strait of Dover, at the narrowest point of the English Channel, which has seen traffic between Britain and the Continent for about 6,000 years. The famous white cliffs of Dover have taken on a wider significance as symbols of the nation as a whole, especially in times of war.

Dover Castle was not the first structure on this hilltop. There may well have been an Iron Age hillfort on the castle site, before the Roman invasion of Britain in AD 43. The Romans built a lighthouse on the heights here to guide ships into the harbour, and a church and some kind of fortification were added by the Saxons. William the Conqueror came here in 1066, immediately after the Battle of Hastings, and strengthened the defences. In the 1180s Henry II remodelled the castle, planning its great tower as a palace in which to entertain great visitors as well as a last redoubt for a strategically important fortress. Building work continued in the first half of the 13th century under King John and Henry III, who completed the successive rings of defensive walls surrounding the great tower. In 1216–17 these defences were twice put to the test when Dover withstood a long siege by French forces.

After the Middle Ages Dover was continuously garrisoned into the 20th century. From the 1740s onwards the medieval banks and ditches were reshaped as the castle was adapted for artillery warfare, and during the Second World War it became the headquarters for the Admiralty's regional command. It was from here that Vice-Admiral Bertram Ramsay organized Operation Dynamo, the evacuation of the British Expeditionary Force from Dunkirk in 1940.

Tour

Dover Castle's spectacular site was an Iron Age hillfort many centuries before the medieval castle was built, and it still contains a Roman lighthouse and an Anglo-Saxon church. Soon after the Conquest in 1066 the Normans built a castle here, and this was developed on a grand scale by Henry II and his successors from 1180 until the 1250s. They created one of the most powerful of all medieval castles. Incorporating a square keep at its heart, it was surrounded by concentric rings of stone walls with regularly spaced wall towers, a combination unprecedented in western Europe.

Since then, the defences of Dover Castle have frequently been adapted and extended to meet the changing needs of warfare, reflecting its strategic importance as the 'key to England'.

FOLLOWING THE TOUR

The tour is divided broadly by period into four main sections: the earliest features on the site, which include the Roman lighthouse and Anglo-Saxon church; the medieval heart of the castle, comprising the great tower and inner bailey; the outer defences, medieval in origin but much adapted in the 18th century; and the later seaward defences, including the wartime tunnels.

The numbers beside the headings highlight key points on the tour and correspond with the small numbered plans in the margins.

Earliest Buildings and Middle Bailey

At the castle's highest point are its two earliest buildings: a Roman lighthouse and an Anglo-Saxon church. This area is also the site of the original medieval castle, which pre-dates Henry II's work and is surrounded by a 13th-century earth bank. An earlier bank below this, dating from the 11th century, was probably part of the late Saxon fortification which William the Conqueror occupied after his victory in 1066.

◼ ROMAN LIGHTHOUSE

At the heart of Dover Castle stands the *pharos* or Roman lighthouse, which probably dates to the first half of the second century AD. This is a unique survival in Britain, which testifies to Dover's importance as a port and fleet base in Roman times. Another lighthouse stood on the high ground on the other side of the valley, on what is now Western Heights: the pair would have formed seamarks by day, and had burning braziers atop them to act as beacons by night. Framing the entrance to the harbour in the Dour estuary, they would have helped sailors to navigate safely into it. They formed a group with a third lighthouse on the far side of the Channel, the Tour d'Odre at Boulogne.

The *pharos* is an octagonal tower built of local flint and ragstone with brick dressings; the tiered arches are also formed of brick. It has five stages, which are most clearly visible on its western side.

The four lower stages are of Roman masonry, with brick levelling courses, and the topmost stage was rebuilt in about 1426–36 by Humphrey, Duke of Gloucester, to adapt it as a belfry for the adjacent church.

A 12th-century reference to a lighthouse keeper at Dover suggests that at this date the *pharos* was still in use. In the 1580s it was roofed, floored and rendered externally to serve as a gunpowder magazine.

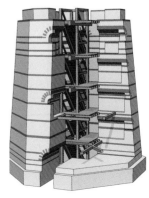

Left: The Roman lighthouse and church of St Mary in Castro, which stand at the highest point within the castle
Below left: A drawing of the lighthouse in 1722 by the antiquary William Stukeley, who noted that the lead had been removed from the roof, leaving 'this rare piece of art and masonry to struggle with the sea air and weather'
Below: A cutaway reconstruction of the Roman lighthouse, showing its probable form when built

Facing page: The central area of the castle, showing the Roman lighthouse and Anglo-Saxon church in the foreground, surrounded by an earth bank, with the inner bailey beyond

2 CHURCH OF ST MARY IN CASTRO

Beside the lighthouse stands the church of St Mary in Castro, the largest and finest Saxon building in Kent. Despite heavy restoration in the 19th century the plan, outer walls and central tower arches are largely original. The size and cruciform plan of the church suggest that it was a minster, a church served by a community of priests. This and its landmark position may indicate that it was a royal foundation. King Eadbald of Kent (d.640) is known to have founded a minster in the 'castrum' of Dover, though it is not clear whether that refers to this site or the Roman fort down in the town (see page 39). The present church, though, has been dated to AD 1000 on comparative, stylistic grounds; we have no other evidence for its date. The church is built of rubble masonry of flint and ragstone, with reused Roman bricks in the quoins (corners) and around the doors and windows.

After the Norman Conquest, the church was maintained to serve the castle community. The vaults over the chancel and crossing, the chancel windows and the north doorway of the nave seem to be from the late 12th or 13th century, and may be contemporary with Henry II's great rebuilding of the castle (see page 40). Documentary sources tell us that sacred relics were kept in the church, and taken out for processions.

The church was restored during a major round of repairs to the castle in 1582, but fell into decay in the late 17th century; by the early 18th century it was a ruined shell. During the Napoleonic Wars it was used as a court for the game of fives (a ball game similar to squash), and then as a coal store. In 1862 it was restored and re-roofed by the architect Sir George Gilbert Scott for use as the garrison church. In 1888 the architect William Butterfield added the upper stage of the tower and decorated the interior of the chancel in his distinctive style, with polychrome wall decoration, a tiled floor and a mosaic altarpiece.

3 EARTH BANK AND MIDDLE BAILEY

The church and lighthouse are surrounded by a great earth bank. Excavations in 1961–2 established that this was raised in the 13th century over an earlier bank and ditch, probably dating from the 11th century. This earlier bank and ditch had been cut through a large Saxon cemetery, an act of sacrilege suggesting a response to an emergency. It may have been a late Saxon development in response to foreign raids, or may represent part of William the Conqueror's works carried out immediately after the Battle of Hastings in 1066. At any rate, this area was surrounded by a line of defences by 1100.

The bank around the church and lighthouse was certainly raised by 1256, when a stone curtain wall, of which traces remain, was built along the top of it. By that stage this oval enclosure was linked to the inner bailey – the heart of the

Above: The vault over the chancel of the church was restored by Sir George Gilbert Scott in 1862, and the walls were later covered with polychrome decoration by William Butterfield
Right: This anonymous early 18th-century view of the inner bailey from the south shows its original elaborate entrance arrangements, from the archway on the right via two further gates to the Palace Gate, seen on the far left

Left: A reconstruction of the castle's main buildings as they may have looked in the 13th century. There were doubtless more buildings within the castle – accommodation for the garrison, barns, stables and storehouses – but we have no evidence for them

A Earth bank
B Middle bailey
C Inner bailey
D Palace Gate
E Barbican
F Colton's Gate

12th-century castle – to the north-west by a series of walls, forming an irregularly shaped 'middle bailey'. It is quite possible that parts of these walls were built earlier, and that the church area, together with the inner bailey area, represents the 11th-century castle. Whatever the case, when the later defences were completed in the mid 13th century, the middle bailey walls provided an intermediate line of defence which covered the

southern approach to the inner bailey. By closing a number of gates in this area, the castle could have been divided into four main compartments.

The surviving section of the linking wall has one major feature: the impressive octagonal gate-tower known as Colton's Gate, which is thought to date from the early 13th century. It was remodelled in the 15th and 16th centuries, and re-roofed by the War Office in about 1900.

Inner Bailey and Great Tower

To the north-west of the church and lighthouse is the inner bailey, which from the 12th century formed the heart of the medieval castle. In the 11th century there may have been a motte or mound here, or possibly a ringwork – an oval enclosure surrounded by a bank and timber palisades. Whatever was here was wiped out in the 1180s, when Henry II (r.1154–89) built the curtain walls and towers of the inner bailey, with its two strongly defended gateways, and the magnificent great tower at its centre.

INNER BAILEY

4 Walls, Towers and Gates

The inner bailey walls with their 14 rectangular mural towers can be dated to the 1180s from a reference in the Pipe Roll (financial records) for 1185–6 to the building of a *cingulum* (belt) around the *turris* (tower), meaning the great tower or keep. The walls are built of rubble masonry faced in Kentish ragstone, with fine dressings of cut Caen stone, a light yellow limestone from Normandy, much of which has been replaced in later repairs. Most of the towers were originally built with only three sides and with no stone wall enclosing them at the rear, like those at contemporary castles such as Framlingham and Windsor. They have since been enclosed by later buildings. Several of them have arrowloops at low level, though it is not clear whether these formed part of the original design.

The inner bailey has two gateways, both protected by flanking towers. To the north is King's Gate: this retains its outer defence works or barbican, which is believed to be contemporary with the gate itself. Palace Gate, to the south, originally had a larger outer barbican, with rather

Above: A sentry standing guard at the barbican leading to King's Gate, the north entrance to the inner bailey, in about 1840

Left: The earliest known view of the castle, drawn probably in the 1570s by the surveyor John Bereblock, whose monogram appears in the lower right corner. It shows the towers of the inner bailey before they were reduced in height in the 18th century, and a covered way linking the great tower and Arthur's Hall

Facing page: The approach to the inner bailey from the north, showing the outer barbican in the foreground. The barbican entrance was offset from the King's Gate beyond it (right) to help protect the gate from assault

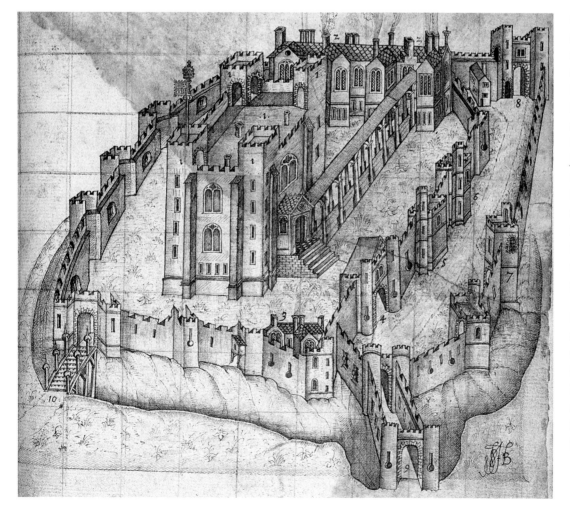

Above: A reconstruction of the great tower and inner bailey as they may have appeared in the mid 13th century, after Henry III had completed his rebuilding of Arthur's Hall and the neighbouring buildings, seen to the right

complex entrance arrangements from its eastern side, but this was demolished in the 18th century. This barbican was in turn linked to the walls of the middle bailey (see reconstruction, page 7).

In 1853 the wall-walks and parapets of the inner bailey towers and walls, which had already lost their original battlements, were remodelled to adapt them for musket fire. The two gateways were also remodelled and given remarkable counterbalanced gates and drawbridges, which still survive. The aim seems to have been to refit the inner bailey as a last redoubt in the event of the rest of the castle being captured.

5 Inner Bailey Buildings

Henry II and his builders evidently intended the inner bailey to house other buildings as well as the great tower. There is documentary evidence that by the early 13th century the structures here included a great hall, a series of royal chambers and a chapel. These buildings were apparently on the north-east side of the bailey, and archaeological excavations here have revealed foundations from the late 12th or early 13th century. These structures were rebuilt for Henry III about 1236–44. Other buildings were added to the complex, and by the late 13th century the

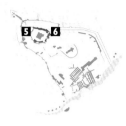

inner bailey housed a brewhouse, a bakehouse and stables, though we do not know their locations. Covered passageways or pentices linked various buildings in the inner bailey together.

These buildings were remodelled in the reign of Edward IV, probably about 1480, with new windows. Their appearance is first depicted in a drawing by the Elizabethan surveyor John Bereblock, likely to have been made in the 1570s, which shows a single long range of buildings on this side of the inner bailey. The three-bay building immediately facing the entrance to the great tower was rebuilt in 1625–6 during the 1st Duke of Buckingham's renovation of the castle (see page 48), with arched windows.

Most of the inner bailey buildings today, however, have a mainly 18th-century appearance, as they were rebuilt as barracks in the 1740s, when Britain was faced with the threat of invasion. No. 5 Keep Yard now houses the Princess of Wales's Royal Regiment and the Queen's Regimental Museum. This was probably built in the mid 13th century as chambers for Henry III and his queen, but was also heavily altered in 1745. The buildings beyond, which now house offices, WCs and education space, are essentially of the 18th century. The smaller building on the other side of the bailey, which now houses the shop, is medieval in origin, and was probably the 'Little Hall' referred to in medieval building accounts.

6 Arthur's Hall

The great hall, which was probably rebuilt about 1236–44 for Henry III, later became known as Arthur's Hall (presumably after the legendary king). The porch-like building to the south represents its original entrance, and is the best-preserved area of medieval work in the bailey. A new kitchen in the south-east corner of the bailey, linked to this hall, and the addition of a chapel over the hall porch probably marked the end of this round of works, about 1244–5.

Excavations in the 1970s revealed some of the medieval features of Arthur's Hall, notably three arched doors of about 1236–40 at its south-east end. These formed part of the traditional arrangement at the low end of a great hall: the central door gave access to a passage to the kitchen, while the doors to either side led to the

pantry (for storing and serving bread), and the buttery (for beer and wine). (From the roof of the great tower the gable of the wall with these doorways, with a blocked window, is visible rising above the 18th-century roof.) In the 1740s Arthur's Hall was rebuilt and had a floor inserted.

Left: The three blocked doors at the south-east end of Arthur's Hall. Their fine masonry may have been carved in the royal workshops at Westminster and brought here ready to be assembled

Below: A king and queen banqueting, depicted in a mid 14th-century French manuscript

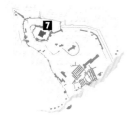

7 GREAT TOWER

Dover Castle's great tower or keep commands its surroundings, and is visible from far out at sea. Built by Henry II in the 1180s, it was the last of the great square keeps that had been built in England since the Norman Conquest. Indeed, its square, turreted design may have been intended as an ancestral statement, echoing the great square keeps built by his grandfather Henry I and great-grandfather William the Conqueror, including the White Tower at the Tower of London, the keeps at Colchester and Norwich, and those at Falaise and Domfront in Normandy. These massive buildings were pre-eminent symbols of royal power.

Henry II was a great builder of keeps. Some of these were to traditional square designs, such as Peveril, in Derbyshire, and Scarborough, and some to cylindrical and polygonal plans, such as Orford in Suffolk, Chilham in Kent, and Gisors in Normandy. Dover's great tower bears closest resemblance to the fine square keep at Newcastle, overseen for Henry in about 1171–8 by the same master-mason, Maurice, at a cost of about £1,000. Dover's great tower, a larger and more elaborate version of that at Newcastle, cost over four times as much – a gigantic sum at that time. It was the most elaborate and expensive, as well as the last, of the Anglo-Norman palace-keeps.

The great tower was certainly designed as an occasional residence or palace for the monarch and his court, or for important visitors, but has only occasionally been used in this way. For most of the Middle Ages it was probably mainly used for storage. In about 1480 Edward IV carried out a major modernization in order to use it as an occasional royal residence: the mullioned windows and fireplaces date from his reign. Henry VIII commissioned a more modest refurbishment in about 1539, and in 1624–5 George Villiers, 1st Duke of Buckingham and constable of the castle, commissioned a further refurbishment of the great tower for palatial use. The anticipated royal visits did not happen, however, and after the Civil War (1642–51) the great tower was used for other purposes: to house French prisoners of war, then as a storehouse, then as barracks, and then as a magazine and powder store. In 1798–9 parabolic brick vaults were built above the second floor in place of the previous timber roofs so that cannon could be mounted on the roof. In the late 19th

century the upper floors of the building were cleared of military stores and opened to the public, with displays of historic armour.

The building has therefore experienced several rounds of alteration since the 12th century. Most recently, in 2008–9, English Heritage carried out a major project to present the interior of the great tower as if the court of Henry II were in residence there (see feature, page 18).

Exterior

The great tower measures 29.9m by 29.3m externally, and 25.5m to the top of its parapets, with walls up to 6.4m thick in places. When built it was faced in grey Kentish ragstone with broad decorative bands of Caen stone from Normandy, used because of the shortage of good building stone in south-east England. It has been patched and refaced on many occasions, and for a long period until the late 19th century it was covered with render. The original surface has thus been badly damaged in places, and today the banding is only clearly visible on the north-west side. Most of the great tower's windows have been recut and relined, some being radically altered in the process. The tower's original appearance is recreated in a model on display in Arthur's Hall.

The great tower is effectively four storeys high, although it has only ever had three full storeys of interiors: the top storey was always a 'dummy' screening a countersunk roof (see page 16). The building's appearance and plan are made more complicated by its forebuilding, which is wrapped around its eastern corner.

Right: Masons building a tower, depicted in a 14th-century manuscript
Below: *The castle keep at Newcastle upon Tyne. Like the great tower at Dover, it has an elaborate forebuilding leading to an entrance at second-floor level*

Facing page: The great tower from the west. The original decorative bands of Caen stone are seen on the north-western facade, to the left. On the other facades they have been largely obliterated by later refacings

Second floor

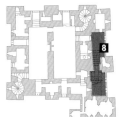

First floor

8 Forebuilding

The forebuilding provides a long and complex entrance route, probably to allow for elaborate welcome ceremonies, as well as to keep unwanted visitors out. Unusually, the entrance stairs rise all the way to the second floor: most Anglo-Norman keeps were entered at first-floor level, and the only English precedent for the arrangement at

Dover is the keep at Newcastle. The steps were originally steeper, as can be seen from the scars left by the original flights in the walls alongside.

The first two flights of steps lead to the doorway of the forebuilding. Originally this had massive timber doors, which would have been removed when the stairs were rebuilt. The first space beyond the doorway was designed as a chapel with an elaborately decorated chancel, for services of welcome and thanksgiving for safe arrival. An altar and simple furnishings have recently been added to emphasize its original purpose. The small room opening off it may have been a sacristy.

A second pair of doors leads to a further flight of stairs, which was originally open to the sky but later roofed over, probably in the late 15th century. The stairs lead to a third gate or doorway, which had a balanced drawbridge before it: the slots for the counterweights that helped to lower and raise it are visible beneath the gate threshold. Once the drawbridge had been lowered the third pair of doors would open and the visitor could pass up a final flight of steps to the top landing (also originally open to the sky) and the entrance to the tower itself. Most of the great tower's doors and windows seem to have been kept very plain, but this entrance doorway was given

Above: The great tower from the south-east, with the forebuilding to the right. The doorway seen opening off the entrance stairs leads directly into the ground floor

Right: The elaborately decorated lower chapel, which opens off the lower vestibule of the forebuilding

decorative colonettes. Off the landing, a simple room has been refurnished and equipped to suggest its likely intended use as a guard chamber. Marks on the wall outside this chamber are the ghost of a stone bench, which was cleverly heated by a chimney flue.

Internal Arrangements

The great tower was carefully planned, with nearly identical suites of rooms on the first and second floors. The second floor is the entrance level, and its interiors would have been higher, rising to timber roofs. This floor was probably intended for the king and the first floor for another person of high rank, whether a royal or noble visitor or another member of the royal family. Each floor has an 'outer' room, towards the forebuilding, and an 'inner' room beyond it, which may be interpreted as a hall and chamber respectively. In the Middle Ages, the hall and the chamber of a royal residence were not just rooms: they were two of the main departments of the royal household, which was the heart of the government and the army.

Around these two main compartments at all four levels there are several mural chambers (rooms contained within the thickness of the walls). Both the spiral stairs in the great tower rise all the way from the ground floor to roof level, so they may both be interpreted as public or common spaces, rather than as a 'public' and 'private' stair.

🟨 Well Chamber

Immediately off the main entrance to the building is the well chamber. This gives access to the great tower's remarkable well, sunk over 122m down into the chalk by the 12th-century builders (that is, as deep as Salisbury Cathedral's spire is high), an astonishing feat of excavation. This seems to prove that even if the building was primarily

Second floor

Left: One of the great tower's two spiral stairs, which rise from the ground floor to the roof. The original stone linings survive throughout, and testify to the fine craftsmanship of the original builders

Below left: An early 16th-century manuscript illustration showing King Henry VIII and Emperor Charles V disputing before Pope Leo X

Henry VIII and Charles V at Dover

In 1520 the castle was still considered a fit place to house an emperor. On Sunday 25 May the Holy Roman Emperor, Charles V, arrived at Dover for a meeting with Henry VIII, and was escorted in a torchlit procession from the harbour to the castle, where the Lord Warden, Sir Edward Poynings, conveyed him to his lodgings.

Henry, who had been waiting at Canterbury, rushed to the castle, and arrived at Dover at two in the morning:
'As sone as the emperor hard of his coming he arose and mett with the king at the staire hedd whereas eyther of them embrased other in arms full lovinglie so that it was aright honorable sight to see the meeting of theis ii excellent princes and their them talked familiarlie a long tyme together.'

Since Edward IV made repairs to the castle in the 1480s, the royal lodgings had been in the great tower. It is therefore very likely that Charles V stayed here, and that he appeared at the top of the forebuilding stairs to greet Henry. Less than a week later, Henry embarked from Dover to meet King Francis I of France at the Field of the Cloth of Gold (see page 46).

CUTAWAY RECONSTRUCTION
OF THE GREAT TOWER IN
ABOUT 1250

A Forebuilding stair

B Lower chapel

C Drawbridge and pit

D King's hall

E King's chamber

F Chapel of Thomas Becket

G First-floor chamber

H Door to ground floor

intended as a palace, it was also designed as a potential refuge if the rest of the castle fell.

10 King's Hall

The first large room entered may originally have been intended as the king's hall. When the court was in residence it would have been used for a variety of purposes – for ceremony and dining, and as a place of meeting and assembly. Numerous members of the household and court would probably have slept here too. At its 'lower' or entrance end a doorway leads to a large garderobe – in effect, the public lavatory. The hall seems to have been carefully planned as a setting for ceremonies, to judge by such features as the entrance stairs descending into the room (to allow important people entering it to be seen), the balcony or gallery overlooking it at third-floor level, and the mysterious blocked archway in the northern wall, which may have been a viewing balcony for important people, or possibly an exit route from a dais at the 'upper' end of the room.

11 Chapel of Thomas Becket

An ante-chamber at the corner of the king's hall leads to a narrow passageway, which gives access to the upper chapel, directly above the chapel in the forebuilding. The narrow access suggests that this was intended for the king and a few others; the little oblong room off to the right may have been a royal pew from where Henry II could have observed and heard services while holding private meetings. The chapel is notable for the richness of its decoration, which is similar in its details to those at Canterbury Cathedral. A great rebuilding of the eastern arm of the cathedral had just been completed in about 1179, providing a magnificent new setting for the shrine of Thomas Becket, the archbishop murdered in his cathedral by four of Henry II's knights in 1170 (see page 40).

12 King's Chamber

The second large room, probably intended as the king's chamber, is similar in size to the hall. The chamber in the 12th and 13th centuries was where the business of government was carried on wherever the king happened to be. In a great medieval household access to this room was more restricted than access to the hall. When the king was in residence this would have been his private

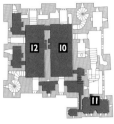

Second floor

apartment, although it was not private by modern standards – in the 12th and 13th centuries the king would have shared his private space with several senior officials and servants. Guards and the more menial attendants probably waited and slept somewhere close to hand.

The small mural chambers opening off this chamber have doubtless served a variety of purposes. They may originally have been intended to house departments of the chamber, such as the wardrobe or scriptorium, but in the 15th century they were converted for more private use, more like modern bedrooms. The window embrasures were widened in the 15th century to allow for the larger two-light windows.

The fireplaces and flues, in both the larger rooms and the mural chambers, were also all inserted in the later 15th century. One of the most surprising and puzzling facts about the great tower

Left: The upper chapel on the second floor of the great tower. The chapel is dedicated to St Thomas Becket, and its richly decorated stonework is similar to contemporary work at Canterbury Cathedral. The newly made window glass, depicting Becket, is based on late 12th-century windows at the cathedral
Below: The king's hall on the second floor, fitted out to give an impression of a royal court in the late 12th century

Recreating Henry II's World

Dover's great tower now gives visitors a unique opportunity to see a fully conceived evocation of a 12th-century royal palace

Henry II crossed the Channel at least 28 times during his 25-year reign, and Dover Castle was rebuilt because it lay at one of the main points of entry to England. He is known to have stayed here on four occasions between April 1185 and the end of his reign, when the great tower was probably complete or nearly so, and he may well have occupied it.

In 2007 English Heritage decided to present the great tower as if Henry and his court were in residence, receiving a great foreign visitor on pilgrimage to Canterbury. The great tower now gives visitors a unique opportunity to see a fully conceived evocation of a 12th-century royal palace.

Displaying the great tower as a 12th-century palatial interior presented a challenge, since few furnishings survive from the period. All the objects on display are of modern manufacture, based on surviving examples or on manuscript illustrations. The need to respect the historic integrity of the building and its later phases of alteration restricted the approach that could be taken – for example, the wall decorations had to be hangings rather than mural paintings. In fact, contemporary wall-paintings in English and French churches reveal that royal and noble residences were indeed often decorated with painted fabric wall-hangings. Military, theological and biblical themes known to have been used in royal decorative schemes of the period were selected, and 12th-century weaves were used for the woollen hangings and other textiles. Doors were reintroduced, following 12th-century models for the joinery and decorative blacksmiths' work.

For the furniture, surviving 12th-century chests, chairs, cupboards and benches were used as models, but some pieces, such as thrones and beds, had to be based on manuscript illustrations. Simple jointing was used throughout. The startlingly bright colour schemes were based on contemporary objects, wall-paintings and manuscripts.

Recreating Henry II's world also involved commissioning many small objects, for most of which there is contemporary evidence. The arms and armour are based on surviving objects or manuscript illustrations, while the pottery was copied from imported wares and Kentish 'Tyler Hill' wares of the 1170s and 1180s. The charters and documents in the scriptorium, off the king's chamber, are written in hands that imitate those of scribes known to have worked in Henry's household, and the neighbouring wardrobe houses clothes and armour based on 12th-century images.

Above: A royal helmet ringed with a crown, made for the great tower
Right: A replica of a book cover, set with precious jewels and an ivory panel depicting the Crucifixion of Christ
Far right: A 'Mappa Mundi', or map of the world, was created on calfskin vellum, following medieval examples and using authentic materials. The map represents the world as it was believed to be in the Middle Ages – circular but flat, and surrounded on all sides by the ocean. East is at the top

In this late 12th-century illumination St Baudemond is shown seated on an X-framed stool with animal heads and feet. Such stools commonly occur in manuscript images, though few actually survive. Several were made for the great tower

The table with columnar legs was based on the example in this late 12th-century manuscript illumination of St Mark the Evangelist. In the 12th century trestle tables were most commonly used, as they could be easily taken down and moved around

The chess set is a resin copy of the famous 12th-century Lewis Chessmen, found in the Outer Hebrides and now mostly in the British Museum. The original pieces, probably made in Scandinavia, consist of elaborately worked walrus ivory and whales' teeth

This late 12th-century wardrobe, or armoire, at the church of St Étienne at Aubazine in France, was used as a model for the one seen above. The Aubazine armoire was probably painted, although its original decoration has been lost

Above: The king's chamber, one of the two main rooms on the second floor, received the richest treatment of all the recreated rooms in the great tower, with elaborate painted hangings showing the signs of the zodiac and the virtues and vices, and brightly coloured furniture. Examples of some of the models used for the furniture and other objects are shown on the left

Roof

First floor

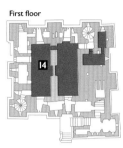

Ground floor

Right: The outer room on the first floor has been furnished and set out as though for a 12th-century banquet
Below: Section through the great tower

is that it originally had no fireplaces, although these were already standard features of Anglo-Norman keeps. Heating could only have been provided with central hearths or braziers, ventilated by the windows. At this date fireplaces were still only used in one or two rooms in high-status buildings, being cleaner and more convenient, if thermally less efficient. The lack of fireplaces does not mean that the great tower was not meant to be occupied and slept in, although it may indicate that the building was intended for brief visits with an emphasis on tradition and ceremonial.

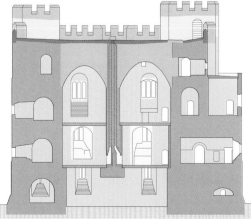

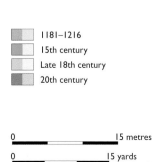

1181–1216
15th century
Late 18th century
20th century

0 _____ 15 metres
0 _____ 15 yards

⓭ Roof

Above the second-floor interiors, the parabolic brick vaults built in the late 18th century are visible. Originally there would have been a steeply pitched countersunk roof (see reconstruction, page 16), contained within and concealed by the third-floor level walls, which themselves housed mural passages. This may seem a strange waste of the whole third storey of the building, but there is clear archaeological evidence for it and this was a fairly standard feature of 11th- and 12th-century keeps, which seem to have been built as much for show, as symbols of lordship and places to entertain great visitors, as for anything else.

It is well worth taking the eastern spiral staircase (through the door immediately to the right of the entrance to the second floor) up to roof level. From here there are spectacular views of the rest of the castle, the town, the Channel and, on a clear day, across to France. The roof platform was created in about 1798–9 to support cannon: some of the original gun positions can still be seen in the paving. Parts of the original battlements were taken down to allow a clear field of fire, and the rest were apparently demolished as recently as the 1930s when the present battlements were created. These do not follow the original pattern.

⒕ First Floor

On the first floor, the layout is almost identical to that of the second, with the same sequence of hall and chamber. It is assumed that it was intended to provide a further suite of accommodation for another member of the royal family or a guest of high rank. Although this level lacks the grand approach afforded to the second floor, it enjoyed a greater degree of security, having no direct access from the entrance stair. Decorative detail on this floor is notably less elaborate, however, and there is no private chapel.

As on the second floor, each room has access to a garderobe contained in the thickness of the north-west wall. There are mural chambers opening off the rooms, most of which are similar in plan and location to those on the second floor. The exceptions are the two rooms that open off the northern spiral stair: these had a water supply, and may have been used for food service in some way. These rooms retain some of their original 12th-century cornices; in most of the interiors these were cut back in the 15th or 16th centuries, when panelling was installed. They are built immediately below the upper landing and forebuilding guardroom.

A notable feature of the first floor is the massive timber framing set into the walls of the hall. This has been dendro-dated to the 1260s, suggesting that it may have been a repair after damage sustained in the siege of 1265 (see page 45). The timberwork is huge, but it is unclear what its original purpose was, as the walls seem more than adequate to support the floor above.

⒖ Ground Floor

The stairs descend to a ground-floor room, which houses a large bread oven. This remarkable feature is undoubtedly original to the building. Medieval bread ovens were heated by being filled with hot charcoal, which was usually supplied from a nearby fireplace; in this case, given the lack of fireplaces in the great tower, the fuel was presumably provided from a central hearth or brazier.

At ground-floor level the two main compartments of the interior are linked by a series of arches in the spine wall. The great tower

originally had just two entrances: the main one via the forebuilding, and a door from the first landing of the entrance steps into this space, which had no fewer than three barred doors to defend it.

This floor was probably used mainly for storage. It is now presented as if Henry II's private kitchen were set up here for a royal visit. There is no specific evidence for this other than the bread oven, which suggests that food preparation could have taken place in the building despite its lack of fireplaces. Visitors emerge via a late 18th-century door into the inner bailey.

Above: Roasting fowl on a spit, from the 14th-century Luttrell Psalter
Below left: A boiling hearth on the ground floor of the great tower, based on scenes from illuminated manuscripts
Below: An aquamanile (jug) in the shape of a lion, based on surviving 13th-century bronze and brass examples

Outer Defences and Battlements Walk

Dover Castle's outer defences enclose an area of over 4ha, making it one of the largest castles in the British Isles. It is likely that the outer curtain walls were begun by Henry II, developed under King John (r.1199–1216), and completed during the minority of Henry III in the 1220s. These fortifications were augmented and adapted for artillery warfare in the 18th and 19th centuries.

The walk around the battlements follows the line of the outer defences and gives splendid views over the castle and its surroundings.

IRON AGE DEFENCES

The castle is surrounded by huge banks and ditches that pre-date the curtain walls, which are cut into the top of the inner banks. There is no evidence for the date of these defences, but they seem likely to be over 2,000 years old and to represent an Iron Age hillfort, comparable to the largest prehistoric earthworks in Britain. On the west side towards the town there is a full inner bank and ditch, and an outer ditch for some of their length; on the east side two ditches run the full length of the earthworks. A gap in the earthworks on this side, near Avranches Tower, also pre-dates the curtain walls. This may represent the site of an entrance to the hillfort.

The Saxon defences and early Norman castle probably only covered the area represented by the inner and middle baileys, rather than the whole Iron Age site. A vast garrison would have been needed to man the whole area of the hillfort.

🔳 NORFOLK TOWERS AND MEDIEVAL TUNNELS

Until 1216–17 the castle's main gate stood at the north-western end of the castle, flanked by strong semicircular towers. Its date is unknown, but it would have been the obvious place for Henry II's engineers to start, as it was overlooked by the higher ground to the north, making it vulnerable to attack. During the siege of 1216 (see feature, page 25), when Prince Louis, heir to the French throne, and his invading army set up their camp and siege engines here, they undermined the gate's eastern tower, and the gap had to be hurriedly shored up by the defenders.

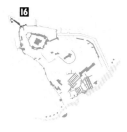

In 1217–21 Hubert de Burgh, the castle's constable, supervised a rebuilding. The collapsed tower was rebuilt as a solid mass of masonry and the gate-passage filled with a new beaked or keel-shaped tower, also built solid. The area was long referred to as the Old Gate, but later became known as the Norfolk Towers, and a new and much stronger gateway, Constable's Gate, was built on the west side of the castle (see page 26).

To guard against future besiegers controlling the high ground to the north, Hubert constructed an extraordinary series of outworks projecting to the north-west. The massive cylindrical St John's Tower was built in the ditch, and on the higher ground to the north, formerly occupied by the barbican, Hubert built an outer spur or bastion of earthworks. Most remarkably, these defences were linked to the castle by a series of tunnels. A deep tunnel burrowed beneath the Norfolk Towers led to St John's Tower, and from there a drawbridge led to another tunnel within the spur itself. This would have enabled the castle's defenders to control the higher ground and frustrate or delay an assault on the Norfolk Towers. The tunnels and

Left: These medieval tunnels originally led from St John's Tower to a detached spur or bastion. They are a unique survival in England
Below: Hubert de Burgh, from Matthew Paris's Historia Anglorum, written in the 1250s. Hubert held the castle during the siege of 1216, and afterwards was in charge of strengthening its defences

Facing page: The castle's western defences, looking north towards Peverell's Gate and Constable's Gate beyond. The curtain walls rise from the top of a steep bank, created by the excavation of the ditch outside. The towers and walls would have risen almost as high as Peverell's Gate, but were reduced in height in the 18th century

Right: The upper floor of the caponier linking St John's Tower to the redan, the gun battery that replaced Hubert de Burgh's spur bastion at the end of the 18th century. The short cannon seen here, known as carronades after the Carron Ironworks Company in Scotland, were designed to fire heavy shot a short distance

spur also housed sally ports or side gates, enabling the garrison to mount counter-attacks in the ditch.

Much of Hubert's tunnels system still exists, and can be seen by visitors. The present entrance is beneath the stone bridge between the Norfolk Towers and the King's Gate barbican. The tunnels are a unique survival, and one of the most remarkable and ingenious pieces of medieval military engineering to survive in Britain.

Hubert's tunnels and spur were partly remodelled in 1756, and then subjected to more sweeping alterations in about 1801–3, to the designs of the military engineer Lieutenant-Colonel William Twiss (see page 31). Twiss recognized that this end of the castle, overlooked by the high ground to the north, still represented the weakest point in its defences. The medieval sally ports were blocked, and an arrow-shaped redan – a massive, detached gun battery – was built on top of Hubert de Burgh's spur. Twiss replaced the medieval tunnel and drawbridge which linked the spur to St John's Tower with a two-storey brick caponier, a heavily built passageway with a bombproof roof and gun ports to either side. He also provided a new sally port, to enable defenders to mount counter-attacks against besiegers in the ditch. This had inner and outer doors, operated from within by a remarkable system of iron levers. Any attackers who got past the outer door could be diverted into an enclosed courtyard, overlooked by firing positions. All this still exists, testimony to the ingenuity of the Georgian engineers.

The Northern Defences

A *Norfolk Towers*
B *St John's Tower*
C *Caponier*
D *Spur*
E *Redan*
F *Entrance to tunnels*

Left: An artist's impression of the great siege of 1216, showing French forces undermining the northern defences of the castle
Below: An attack on a medieval castle, showing miners demolishing the base of a tower, from a manuscript of about 1240

The Great Siege of 1216–17

In 1216–17 Dover Castle withstood a now legendary siege during the civil war between King John and his English barons.

The rebel barons, provoked by what they saw as John's tyrannical rule, had invited Prince Louis of France to assume the English Crown (see page 43). Louis landed in north Kent in May 1216 and quickly secured London and much of southern England. In July he laid siege to Dover, which if captured would have given him control of the Channel's shortest crossing point. The castle was being held for the king by Hubert de Burgh, Justiciar of England and constable of the castle, with a force of 140 knights.

Prince Louis directed the thrust of his attack at the castle's most vulnerable point, the north gate, and set up camp on the higher ground immediately to the north. The defenders had tried to compensate for this weakness by building a timber barbican or outwork to defend the gatehouse, but the French bombarded the walls with stone-throwing engines, tunnelled underneath the barbican, and soon captured the outer defences. Louis' miners then set to work undermining the gatehouse itself. Its eastern tower collapsed, but fierce hand-to-hand fighting by the garrison prevented the castle from being stormed. According to a later chronicler, 'the people inside drove them out with great vigour, and then closed up the place where the walls had fallen, with great timbers, and cross-beams, and palisades of oak trunks'.

After the failure of the assault Louis struck a truce on 14 October. Almost immediately afterwards, on 18 October, King John died. The following May Louis resumed the siege, bringing a massive siege engine. But this time the defenders had little to fear: French defeats at the battle of Lincoln in May and at sea off Sandwich in August compelled Louis and his English allies to accept a settlement.

Dover remained uncaptured, although badly damaged. The siege had laid bare the weakness of the castle's northern defences, and the extraordinary defensive system begun by Hubert de Burgh soon afterwards was designed to remedy this.

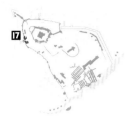

c.1200
1221–30
1805
1883

0   15 metres
0   15 yards

🔟 CONSTABLE'S GATE

From the Norfolk Towers, the curtain wall runs due south to the Constable's Gate, incorporating three towers – the Crevecoeur, Godsfoe and Treasurer's towers. A hall is believed to have run between the first two towers in the Middle Ages, doubtless part of the accommodation for the garrison. Beyond them are the 19th-century deputy constable's stables, and the Constable's Gate. Although most visitors today enter Dover Castle by the relatively modest-looking Canon's Gate of 1797, at the south end of the western curtain, Constable's Gate has been the castle's main entrance since Hubert de Burgh built it in

1217–21, in response to the collapse of the old gate at the north end of the castle.

To create the new gate, Hubert knocked an archway through an earlier D-shaped mural tower, and added a large new tower which projected into the moat in the shape of two Ds back-to-back. This rises from an immensely high battered (sloping) base because of the great depth of the moat. New semicircular towers were built to either side, to protect the flanks. A solid bridge structure was built spanning the moat, with a gate or barbican on its outer side, and beneath the new gatehouse a tunnel was dug down through the chalk leading to a sally port into the ditch, beneath the bridge.

A fine residence was built above the gate for the constable, the official in charge of the castle, who at the time was Hubert himself. Hubert was also Lord Warden of the Cinque Ports, a federation of five Channel ports charged with the defence of the coast (see page 28), and from this time on the two offices were usually combined. Constable's Gate represents the start of a tradition of grand residential gatehouses in English castle design; it remained the official residence of the Lord Warden of the Cinque Ports until 1708, and is still the official home of the deputy constable.

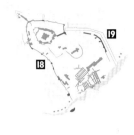

Above right: The Barons of the Cinque Ports had numerous privileges, including the right to carry the canopy over the new king at his coronation, as seen in this 15th-century illustration of the coronation procession of Richard I in 1189

Below: Canon's Gate, seen from inside the castle in a watercolour of 1809 by Captain John Durrant. This new entrance to the castle was created by William Twiss in 1797 to make it easier to move troops between castle and town. The casemates beside the gate passage were built as guardrooms

The Cinque Ports
The five (cinque) ports of Hastings, Romney, Hythe, Sandwich and Dover first banded together in the 11th century to provide ships and men to defend the coast and protect cross-Channel trade. In return for this work, vital to the Crown before a permanent royal navy existed, they were granted substantial privileges. The post of Lord Warden was created by Henry III in an attempt to exert more royal control over this powerful body. From the later 13th century the federation was administered from Dover Castle.

In the late 19th century the deputy constable was an important man, the general commanding the south-eastern military district of England, and the residence was no longer deemed adequate. A handsome wing was added in 1883–4 by the architect R Dawson Scott, together with a coach house and stables immediately to the north.

18 WESTERN CURTAIN

The western curtain walls extend south from Constable's Gate all the way to the cliff edge, strengthened by another seven mural towers which rise from impressive battered bases and have a variety of shapes. Their names commemorate the baronies that owed castle-guard (a fixed period of service each year) to Dover, and the manors which were responsible for the towers' maintenance. In about 1800 this stretch of the walls was reduced in height and earth banks were piled up behind them by Lieutenant-Colonel (later Brigadier-General) William Twiss, to allow the walls to bear cannon and make them more resistant to artillery attack. The walls are still impressive, but would have been more so before these changes.

Beyond the semicircular Queen Mary's Tower, to the south of Constable's Gate, is Peverell's Gate. From here a length of wall once ran to join the inner bailey near Palace Gate, creating an internal division within the castle. Both these towers have especially deep arrowloops. To the south is a long stretch of curtain wall with three closely spaced semicircular towers, Gatton's, Say's and Hurst's towers, all rising from high, battered bases. Further south after a gap is Fulbert of Dover's Tower, which is a simpler, square shape. This stretch of wall has been attributed to the 1220s on the grounds that the towers are of a sophisticated form, but there is no documentary evidence for this date, and the shape of the towers is not in itself conclusive dating evidence. Analysis of the masonry and mortar may one day shed further light on the date and sequence of construction of the outer curtain walls.

Further down the hill and backing onto the curtain wall is a handsome 18th-century brick building, the Cinque Ports prison, which mainly housed debtors. To its south, also backing onto the curtain wall, is a plain stone-faced building of about 1912, built as the Royal Garrison Artillery Barracks and now housing archaeological stores. The pretty little building with overhanging eaves on the left of the path was a meat store for the garrison, built in 1894. Below it on the left is a substantial Victorian Gothic building, built in 1868 as the garrison's canteen and recreation rooms and later used as the Regimental Institute and then the NAAFI (Navy, Army and Air Force Institute).

This now houses the main restaurant and castle offices. On the right of the entrance road is a brick magazine, and on the left is the entrance to the wartime tunnels (see page 34).

Canon's Gate, now the main vehicle entrance to the castle, was cut through the wall by William Twiss in 1797. The bridge in front of it is actually a two-tier caponier, a covered passage housing galleries from which the defenders could cover the castle ditch with fire. A square bastion built in the ditch in the reign of Henry VIII is visible from the bridge. The castle's western defences were continued by the construction of Moat's Bulwark, at the foot of the cliff; this was first built in 1539–40 but remodelled in the 1750s.

19 EASTERN DEFENCES

The eastern defences are also best seen by starting from the Norfolk Towers. The brick buildings lining the curtain wall behind the towers are casemated barracks (built within brick vaults for protection), dating from William Twiss's modernization of the castle between about 1797 and 1810. The brick vaults supported a platform for guns overlooking the vulnerable northern end of the castle.

From here, a straight section of curtain wall runs eastwards, punctuated by square mural towers. Earth banks were piled up behind these walls in 1755–6 to strengthen them against artillery attack. In the middle of this section is the Fitzwilliam Gate, named after a late 15th-century deputy constable: unusually, there is documentary evidence to suggest a date for it, of 1227. It has a distinctive design with three beak-shaped towers. Like Constable's Gate it had accommodation above it, though this is now ruinous. The gate was built with an outwork, a covered passage spanning the moat and housing steps rising to the gate. During the Napoleonic period this was rebuilt with a caponier beneath it from which troops could direct fire along the ditch. The present steps and parapets are a rebuilding of the 1930s.

At the north-east corner of the castle is the polygonal Avranches Tower, part of the original curtain wall and probably dating from the late 12th or early 13th century. The tower covers the angle

Above: The castle from the east. The concentric medieval defences are clearly visible, as are the earthworks of the later artillery defences

Right: Avranches Tower, a powerful polygonal structure built in the late 12th or early 13th century to control an angle in the eastern defences. Its two tiers of arrowloops make it an important landmark in the history of castle design

Below right: One of the arrowloops of the Avranches Tower, seen from the inside. The triple loops enabled defenders to cover the ground on all sides of the tower in safety

Below: A crossbowman, depicted in an early 14th-century manuscript. The short arrowloops of the Avranches Tower were designed for crossbows rather than longbows

where the curtain wall turns southwards, and was perhaps so designed to protect a gap in the existing earthworks, which may represent the entrance to an Iron Age hillfort, and was a potential weak point in the defences. The tower has two tiers of arrowloops in splayed groups of three. If, as seems likely, they are medieval, they appear to be unprecedented in English castle military architecture.

From here the curtain wall turns south for a short distance to Pencester Tower. To the left

William Twiss (1745–1827)

Much of Dover Castle's present appearance is due to the work of William Twiss during the Napoleonic Wars. Earlier in his career he served as an officer in the Royal Engineers, working on the defences of Portsmouth, Plymouth and Gibraltar, and later in North America (during the War of Independence) and then in Canada.

Twiss returned to England in 1792, and served as senior Royal Engineer responsible for the southern military district. Fears of invasion by revolutionary France prompted a huge campaign of defensive works in the area, which kept Twiss busy until his retirement in 1809. As well as his work at Dover Castle, he developed the fortifications on the Western Heights opposite (see page 50), and had a major role in the development of the chain of Martello Towers along the south coast.

Left: William Twiss retired to Bingley in the West Riding of Yorkshire, and died there in 1827. His monument in All Saints' Church, Bingley, shows his portrait against a Martello Tower, a reference to those that he helped to build along the south coast

Below: A photograph of the Officers' New Barracks, taken soon after their construction in the 1850s

there is a dramatic view along the deep outer ditch, which was lined with brick in the 1850s. A narrow tunnel leads past the remains of Pencester Tower up to Bell Battery, which was added in 1756 to house cannon to cover the approach along the Deal Road.

Historic plans show that the medieval curtain wall on the east side was less strongly defended than the western curtain, having just five mural towers from Pencester Tower to the cliff edge. The wall and towers probably still exist in part but are completely invisible, having been buried on both sides by the massive earth banks raised by William Twiss between about 1797 and 1800. The earthworks on this side were already huge, with a double line of banks and ditches. Twiss was not satisfied, however, and added four outworks to them: Horseshoe Bastion, Hudson's Bastion, East Arrow Bastion and East Demi-Bastion, the last-named being just north of the cliff edge. These detached bastions were linked to the castle by tunnels, which still exist. They housed guns that allowed the eastern slopes to be covered with flanking fire.

The battlements walk leads along the top of the ramparts, past early 19th-century gun emplacements; the earth-covered structures are expense magazines, which housed ready supplies of gunpowder. Further south are four circular bases that supported Second World War light anti-aircraft guns, and near the cliff edge are two small brick observation posts and a naval radar station, again from the Second World War. From here steps lead down to the main approach road. On the far side is the impressive Victorian Gothic bulk of the Officers' New Barracks, designed by Anthony Salvin and built in 1856–8.

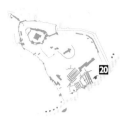

20

Left: The interior of the Fire Command Post within Admiralty Look-out, drawn by the war artist Anthony Gross in 1941

Below: A modern statue of Admiral Sir Bertram Home Ramsay (1883–1945) by Steve Melton, close to the entrance to his underground headquarters in the tunnels at Dover Castle. Admiral Ramsay masterminded the evacuation of Dunkirk in 1940 from these headquarters

Facing page: Admiralty Look-out, which housed a Fire Command Post and the Port War Signal Station, with the town and harbour below

Seaward Defences and Wartime Tunnels

The seaward defences at Dover Castle are entirely post-medieval. Throughout most of the castle's life the cliff itself needed no defences, but from the mid 19th century onwards the development of more powerful guns and the need to protect the harbour below led to new installations on the cliff edge.

The cliffs at Dover Castle also have another dimension, in the shape of a huge underground complex carved out of the chalk cliffs during the Napoleonic Wars. Originally built as barracks, these tunnels were adapted during the Second World War and played a vital role in Britain's war effort, most notably as the command centre for the Dunkirk evacuation.

20 CLIFF-EDGE DEFENCES AND ADMIRALTY LOOK-OUT

In the mid 19th century a revolution in gun-making made all previous generations of artillery obsolete. The castle had to be able to defend itself against the new generation of naval artillery, and in 1871–4 four batteries of heavy guns were added to the seaward side of the castle. East Demi-Bastion, just outside the east curtain wall,

was re-equipped with two new guns, while three new batteries – Shoulder of Mutton Battery (south of Canon's Gate in the western ditch), and Hospital Battery and Shot Yard Battery (on the cliff edge inside the castle) were constructed to carry further weapons.

The flat area of ground beside the statue of Admiral Ramsay is the site of the 19th-century garrison hospital. The surviving structure here, known as Admiralty Look-out (a name that probably emerged after the Second World War), was based on Hospital Battery. In 1905 the battery was converted into a Fire Command Post to monitor naval movements in the Channel, and in 1914 the Admiralty extended the structure with an upper floor to house its main regional signal station, which was moved here from the Western Heights. From here, ship movements in the harbour were controlled.

Admiralty Look-out played a significant role in both world wars. The concrete platform above it was added in 1941, to protect it from aerial attack. Its interiors have been restored and partially fitted out with real and reproduction objects to reflect their appearance in 1918.

21 WARTIME TUNNELS

Right: Prime Minister Winston Churchill on the balcony of the Casemate level tunnels during a tour of defences on 28 August 1940. Enemy air attacks were in progress at the time, and two German bombers were seen to crash into the sea

Below: A wartime photograph of the operating theatre in the underground hospital in Annexe level, the upper level of the tunnels which was added in 1941–2

21 WARTIME TUNNELS

During the Revolutionary and Napoleonic Wars with France (1793–1815), Britain faced the most urgent threat of invasion since the Spanish Armada in 1588. The defence of Dover became a national priority, and William Twiss had the task of providing accommodation for a garrison of several thousand men, in a castle which was already crowded. He responded by designing perhaps the most extraordinary barracks ever built in Britain, in a series of vast tunnels, cut out of the chalk about 20m below the level of the cliff-top, and probably capable of housing up to 2,000 men. At the cliff edge they were given brick facades and an entrance gallery, also cut through the rock.

By the end of the 19th century the tunnels had probably fallen out of use. In 1938, however, with war with Germany looming and the new threat of bombing all too evident, they found a new and vital role as a secure naval headquarters, responsible for command of the Channel coast. It was from here that Vice-Admiral Bertram Ramsay and his staff planned and supervised Operation Dynamo, the rescue of allied troops from Dunkirk between 26 May and 3 June 1940.

Pressure on space during the war led both to the expansion of the original Napoleonic tunnels,

which became known as Casemate level, and to the excavation of two further levels of tunnels. Annexe level, dug in 1941–2, was a little higher than the original Napoleonic tunnels, and served partly as a secure hospital and partly as emergency dormitory accommodation. By 1942 a decision had been made to locate a combined headquarters here for all three services – army, navy and air force – and in 1942–3 a further, larger network of tunnels, codenamed Dumpy level, was dug about 15m lower down. This was completed by May 1943.

After the war the headquarters was closed, but the onset of the Cold War gave the tunnels a final and strange new lease of life: they were adopted by the Home Office as one of 12 emergency Regional Seats of Government which would take charge of the country in the event of nuclear attack. Large sums of money were spent adapting Dumpy level as the heart of the operation, equipping it with generators, plant, furniture and stores of all kinds. This remained in place until 1984.

In 1990 English Heritage reopened Casemate level to commemorate the fiftieth anniversary of the Dunkirk evacuation. Casemate and Annexe levels are now both open to the public, and are presented to evoke the period in British history when Dover Castle was once again at the heart of the defence of the realm.

A separate guide to the wartime tunnels and the castle's role in the Second World War is available.

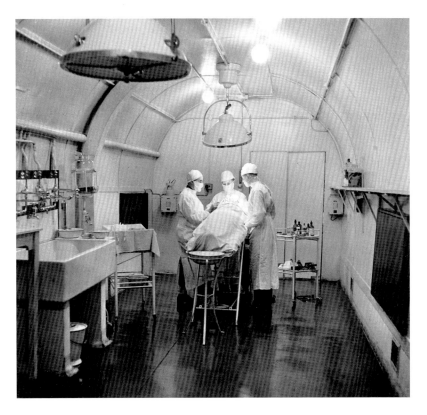

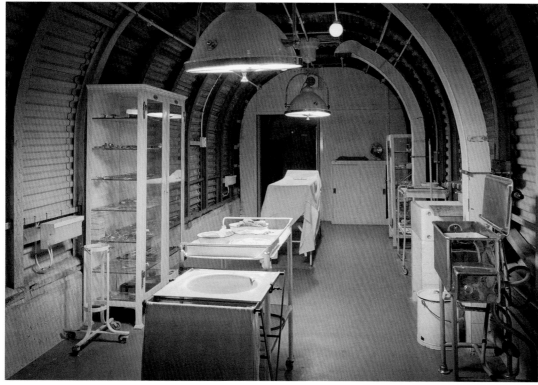

Above: The reconstructed coastal artillery operations room within the tunnels, which was part of Dover Combined Headquarters from 1943
Left: A recreated operating theatre in Annexe level today (compare with the wartime photograph opposite)

History

Dover Castle has been continuously garrisoned for over nine centuries, from the Norman Conquest until the departure in 1958 of the last military unit to be stationed here.

Long before Henry II built the great stone castle, this spectacular site may have been occupied by an Iron Age hillfort; later it housed a Roman lighthouse and a Saxon fortified settlement. The medieval fortress created by Henry II and his Plantagenet successors was severely tested during an epic siege in 1216–17, when it stood almost alone against a powerful invasion force led by Prince Louis of France. Afterwards, Henry III completed the castle's defences, making it the strongest fortress in medieval England.

After the Middle Ages the castle hosted royal visitors, including Henry VIII, Elizabeth I and Henrietta Maria, Charles I's future queen. From 1740 until 1945 its defences were successively updated in response to almost every major European war in which Britain was involved.

BEFORE THE CASTLE
The Formation of the English Channel

Looking across the Channel from the castle on a clear day, another high chalk cliff is visible: this is Cap Blanc Nez, between Calais and Boulogne. Half a million years ago, during a cold period when sea levels were much lower than now, Britain and the North Sea were part of a huge land mass, and a chalk ridge stretched from what is now Kent to northern France. As glaciers melted, a vast freshwater lake, fed by rivers such as the Rhine and Thames, formed to the north of this natural dam. Eventually, between about 400,000 and 100,000 years ago, a 'megaflood' carved a breach through the soft chalk, which would have widened swiftly. In the era since the last ice age sea levels rose again, making this river valley into the English Channel. The cliff on which Dover

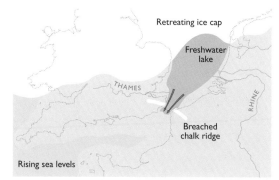

Castle stands and the white cliffs to its east represent one side of this 23-mile breach, and Cap Blanc Nez the other.

Britain remained linked to continental Europe by the area to the north-east, known as Doggerland, until about 6000 BC, when rising sea levels finally made Britain an island. During the Neolithic era (about 4100–2400 BC) cross-Channel traffic began, probably in the Dover area, the Channel's narrowest point. It seems likely, from the remarkable discovery in 1992 of a plank-sewn boat, dated to about 1550 BC, that there was traffic across the Strait of Dover during the Bronze Age (about 2400–800 BC). Known as the Dover Boat, this is now on display at the Dover Museum.

Iron Age Hillfort

Pottery evidence reveals that there was regular cross-Channel trade throughout the Iron Age (about 800 BC–AD 43), and it is likely that new settlers came from the Continent as well. Dover Castle's medieval curtain walls sit on top of massive earth ramparts and ditches, which probably originated as a great Iron Age hillfort. If this is so, the site of the castle has been occupied for over 2,000 years.

The banks and ditches enclose over 4ha, which would make this one of two large Iron Age hillforts in east Kent, the other being at Bigbury,

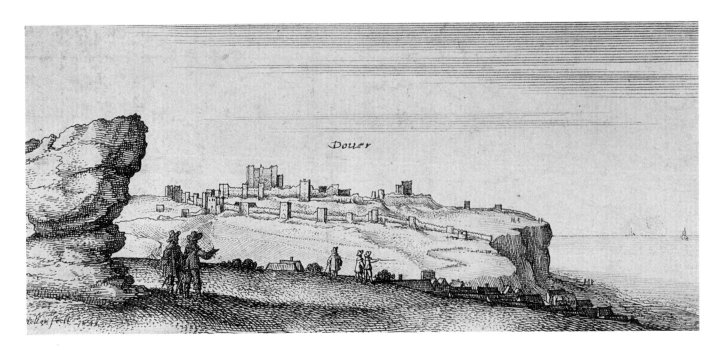

Dover

Above: An engraving of 1645 of Dover Castle from the Western Heights, by the Czech artist Wenceslaus Hollar. On the left is the lump of masonry known as the Bredenstone, which is all that survives of the second Roman lighthouse. Constables and Lords Warden of the Cinque Ports used to be sworn in on this spot

Right: The main Roman sites of Dover. The Roman harbour lay within the Dour estuary

Below: The outline of a contemporary lighthouse, scratched on a Romano-British floor tile. The two lighthouses at Dover were probably of a similar design

south of Canterbury. Such hillforts were used as tribal defences from about the sixth or fifth century BC until the Roman invasion of AD 43. Some were occupied permanently, while others were places of refuge.

ROMAN DOVER

When the Emperor Claudius sent the forces that were to conquer Britain in AD 43, the commander Aulus Plautus landed at Richborough, further north up the coast near modern Sandwich, and Richborough was initially the principal port of Roman Kent. In the first half of the second century, however, a fleet, the Classis Britannica, was

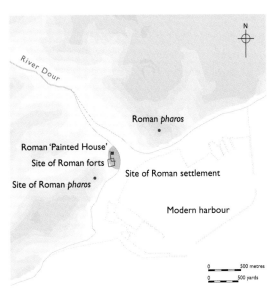

River Dour

N

Roman *pharos*

Roman 'Painted House'
Site of Roman forts

Site of Roman *pharos*

Site of Roman settlement

Modern harbour

0   500 metres
0   500 yards

formed to patrol the Channel, and Dover was selected as its base on the British side, with Boulogne on the French side. The port of Richborough was now overtaken by Dover, whose harbour on the Dour estuary, where Market Square is now, had probably been in use since prehistoric times. Traces of a massive Roman harbour wall have been found beneath the town. A rectangular stone fort laid out on the south side of Dover's harbour in about AD 115–20, but never completed, and a second fort built on a similar site in about AD 130–40, which was completed and occupied, were probably linked to the harbour. The *pharos* or lighthouse in the castle, and another that once stood on the other side of Dover, were clearly intended to act as beacons, guiding shipping into the port in between. They are thought to date from the early second century AD.

Early in the third century the Classis Britannica abandoned the fort at Dover. In the 270s a new fort was built over the levelled remains at its north-east corner. This was one of several forts built around this time to improve the coastal defences and communications of Britain. Sections of its massive walls have been traced by excavation.

North of the fort there was an extensive civilian settlement, which probably pre-dated it. In the 1970s the remains of the 'Painted House' – a large and finely decorated building thought to have been a *mansio*, or official guesthouse for travellers – were discovered just north of the Roman fort.

SAXON DOVER

We know nothing for certain about Dover's history in the centuries immediately after the Roman withdrawal. It seems likely that its harbour remained in use. Kent in the sixth and seventh centuries was the most powerful of the English kingdoms, ruled from Canterbury by its own line of kings. When St Augustine landed in Thanet in 597, King Æthelberht and Queen Bertha welcomed him, and the people of Kent were the first of the English to convert to Christianity.

In the seventh century Eadbald, king of Kent (d.640), founded a minster church for 22 canons in the 'castrum' of Dover. We do not know if this refers to the Roman fort in the town or the hillfort on the headland, but in about 696 the minster was moved to the church of St Martin in the town. The kingdom of Kent was absorbed into that of Wessex in the eighth century. Nevertheless, Dover remained important as a port: a mint was established here, probably in the reign of Æthelstan (924–39).

The church of St Mary in Castro at the heart of Dover Castle has been dated to the 10th or early 11th century on stylistic grounds (see page 6). Its size suggests that there was a substantial community around it on the hill, an idea that seems to be borne out by the existence of a large Saxon cemetery to its south, which was partly excavated in the 1960s and found to contain the graves of men, women and children. This suggests that there was a defensive enclosure or burgh up on the hill within the Iron Age earthworks by the time of the Norman Conquest in 1066, but we know little else about it. In 1051 Count Eustace of Boulogne made a raid on Dover, when he and his men 'went up to the town', according to a contemporary chronicler, and killed more than 20 inhabitants: the wording suggests that this may refer to the castle site.

THE NORMAN CONQUEST

At the Battle of Hastings on 14 October 1066 William, Duke of Normandy, and his army defeated the Saxon army led by King Harold. Afterwards William turned east to Dover, taking the town on 21 October and burning it. He remained there for eight days and built fortifications, before moving on to Canterbury and then London for his coronation on Christmas Day.

Dover already had defences of some kind; William doubtless wanted to secure them

immediately after his victory in order to secure the port. We have no evidence of what they looked like, or what William did here. The banks and ditches from the supposed Iron Age hillfort were probably here, but would have required a vast garrison to man them. It seems likely that the 11th-century castle was smaller than the hillfort, probably enclosing the area around the church and perhaps the site of the inner bailey as well.

The Domesday survey of 1086 makes no reference to the castle, though it does make it clear that the town of Dover had legal privileges in return for providing ship-service to the king. These arrangements were later formalized, with Dover being recognized as one of the 'Cinque Ports', together with Sandwich, Hastings, Romney and Hythe, responsible for providing ships to defend the Channel coast. The Domesday survey also makes it clear that the town had suffered during the Norman Conquest: 20 years later its taxable value 'could not be reckoned'.

The castle was evidently important, because in the mid 12th century nine baronies were established in south-eastern England, one of them to support the constable of Dover, and the other eight to owe knight-service to provide for its defence on a permanent basis (see feature, page 45). There are only a few parallels in England for such elaborate provisions being made to support a castle's defence.

Above: A coin of Eadbald, a seventh-century king of Kent who founded a church at Dover

Below: A scene from the Bayeux Tapestry, showing Duke William raising his helmet to show that he has not been killed or wounded, with Eustace of Boulogne to his right. Eustace is known to have raided Dover twice, in 1051 and again in 1067, after the Norman Conquest, when he and a group of Kentish rebels made an unsuccessful attempt to seize the castle

Right: A near-contemporary portrait of Henry II, showing his red hair and beard, from the manuscript of Gerald of Wales's account of Henry's conquest of Ireland
Below right: The murder of Thomas Becket, Archbishop of Canterbury, by four of Henry II's household knights, depicted in a late 12th-century manuscript

HENRY II AND THE GREAT REBUILDING

Dover Castle owes more to King Henry II (r.1154–89) than to any other individual. He initiated the rebuilding of the castle in the 1180s, and his personality remains stamped upon it. Henry inherited the English throne in 1154, but he was also the Duke of Normandy and the Count of Anjou in France, and by his marriage to Eleanor of Aquitaine in 1153 he had gained her vast duchy, covering most of south-west France. His huge dominions, sometimes known as the Angevin Empire, had come together by a series of accidents, but Henry was a brilliant ruler and became the most powerful monarch of his age.

Dover's role in his empire changed due to an unforeseeable series of events. In 1162 Henry made his chancellor and close friend Thomas Becket the Archbishop of Canterbury. The result was one of the great confrontations of medieval history, with Becket seeing himself as a champion of the independence of the Church from royal interference. He spent the years 1165–70 in exile in France, but when the pope negotiated his return to England in 1170, the row broke out afresh. Henry II was wintering in Normandy. At Becket's latest provocation, Henry's volcanic temper got the better of him, and he exploded with rage, complaining that his court had allowed him to be insulted by a 'low-born priest'. Four of his household knights were spurred into action,

departing in secret and arriving in Canterbury on 29 December. They probably intended to arrest Becket for treason, but their hot blood and the archbishop's refusal to take any steps for his own protection led to tragedy: they murdered him in his own cathedral. The four knights fled into exile; none of them was ever punished for the deed.

The murder shocked Europe, and Becket swiftly came to be regarded as a martyr. Within months, miracles were being reported at his tomb and pilgrims were coming to Canterbury; he was made a saint in 1173. Henry refused to acknowledge any of this, until a great rebellion convulsed his empire in 1173–4. He needed the Church's forgiveness and support, and was forced to make a humiliatingly public penitential visit to the shrine, where the monks ceremonially flogged him. By a remarkable coincidence, on the very next day his enemy William II of Scotland, who had invaded Northumberland, was captured by Henry's forces at Alnwick. God appeared to have accepted the king's penitence. From then on Becket's shrine had royal recognition – and its fame was spreading overseas. In 1179 Louis VII of France himself arrived at Dover. His 15-year-old son (and successor), Philip Augustus, was gravely

parliut

Left: An early 14th-century manuscript illustration of a horse-drawn carriage entering the gates of a city. The royal household was almost constantly on the move
Below: The reverse of the royal seal of Henry II, showing the king on horseback

The King's Household

Henry II's court and household formed one of the great centres of power in Europe, but he was renowned for being constantly on the move. His household, numbering several hundred people, was based on five main departments which looked after not only the king himself, his money and portable goods, but also the governance of the realm. The chapel and chancery provided for the household's spiritual life, and also produced the written documents needed for government. The steward's department looked after the hall, kitchens and supply of food. The chamber represented the inner household, which looked after the king, his money and portable goods, and provided the inner workings of his government. The constable headed the household knights, who protected the king and formed the core of the royal army. The marshal was responsible for the outside departments, including the stables, transport, and the whole hunting establishment, as well as for discipline within the household.

Around this core, there was doubtless a fluctuating population of visiting nobles and clerics, foreign envoys, young men being educated at court, merchants, tradesmen, servants, prostitutes, petitioners, and beggars. The court was an overwhelmingly male place, and this was especially so in the 1180s when the queen, Eleanor of

Aquitaine, was effectively imprisoned at Old Sarum and Winchester for her role in the rebellion against the king in 1173–4.

Passing by in long processions of slow-moving wagons, riders and pedestrians, the royal household would have presented one of the most remarkable sights in the medieval world. Feeding, housing and transporting the court and household were major undertakings, which over time would have strained the resources of almost any part of the country. This was of course one of the reasons why the household travelled around so much.

Passing by in long processions of slow-moving wagons, riders and pedestrians, the royal household would have presented one of the most remarkable sights in the medieval world

ill, and in this supreme crisis the king felt the need to pray at Becket's shrine. His arrival in England took Henry completely by surprise, forcing him to make an overnight dash to meet Louis in Kent, accompany him to Canterbury, and escort him back to Dover.

Dover was a strategically important castle, but not somewhere the king would usually have expected to spend much time. It was not on his normal route to France (which was via Portsmouth or Southampton), and Kent had no royal forest to provide hunting and help feed the court. Yet Henry began a huge rebuilding of the castle in 1180, the year after Louis VII's visit. Between about 1180 and 1189 he spent more than £6,000 on it, a vast sum, which made it by far the most expensive castle project of his reign in England.

It is very likely that the reason for this huge undertaking was the fact of the new pilgrimage route to Canterbury, which was now internationally recognized. Henry had to come to terms with it, but he also had to assert his authority somehow, and it seems that he needed a magnificent setting here in which to receive important visitors to Becket's shrine.

THE REIGNS OF RICHARD I AND KING JOHN

When Henry II died in France in 1189, work was still in progress at Dover. The great tower and inner bailey curtain walls were probably complete, and it is likely that work had started on building the outer curtain walls. Henry II was succeeded by the elder of his surviving sons, Richard I 'Lionheart', whose principal concern on his succession was to raise the funds to lead the Third Crusade in Palestine. Work nevertheless continued at Dover, where another £600 was spent in 1189–91.

Richard sailed from Dover for France in 1190, and did not return to England until 1194. In these years Philip II Augustus of France, who had succeeded his father, Louis VII, in 1180, was seeking to restore the power of the French monarchy, and the Angevins with their great French dominions were the main obstacle in his path. When Richard I was unexpectedly killed while besieging a castle in south-western France in 1199, and was succeeded by his much less able brother John, Philip saw his chance. Between 1202 and 1205, by a mixture of legal technicality, political intrigue and military force, and greatly helped by John's incompetence and appalling mistakes, Philip progressively conquered Touraine, Anjou, Maine and Normandy.

With the loss of Normandy, for the first time in 140 years England was faced by a hostile power on the other side of the Channel. John was obliged to make the defence of the Channel coast an urgent priority, and he established the first royal fleet between about 1205 and 1215. Dover was now potentially a frontier fortress, and John spent over £1,000 on the castle's defences, probably completing the outer curtain walls in these years. They would soon be put to the test.

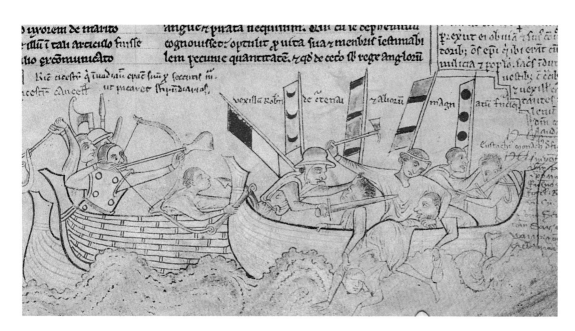

Left: The Battle of Sandwich Bay in August 1217, at which Hubert de Burgh's ships decisively defeated French reinforcements, ending all hopes of a French victory on land. From the Chronica majora *by Matthew Paris (d.1259)*

Below: The siege of Chinon in 1204–5, at which Hubert de Burgh gained fame for his stubborn (though ultimately unsuccessful) defence of the castle against the French king; from a 14th-century French manuscript

HUBERT DE BURGH AND THE GREAT SIEGE

John's government became notorious for its harshness and oppressive taxation. In 1215 this led to a broad-based rebellion, headed by most of the English barons and the Church, which forced John to sign the Great Charter of Liberties or Magna Carta. The agreement broke down the following autumn, when John repudiated the charter and the rebellion broke out anew. By this time, two-thirds of the English barons had gone over to the rebel side: they wrote to Philip Augustus asking for his support and offering the English Crown to his son, Prince Louis. Philip saw an opportunity to destroy the Angevins completely and sent an expeditionary force, commanded by Louis, which landed in north Kent in May 1216. In July Louis turned south to besiege Dover, realizing that its capture would give him control over the port at the Channel's shortest crossing point: as the historian Matthew Paris later put it, the castle had become the 'key to England'.

John had entrusted Dover Castle to the care of Hubert de Burgh, one of his most loyal and effective supporters. Hubert had distinguished himself by his year-long (though ultimately unsuccessful) defence of the chateau of Chinon in Touraine against Philip Augustus's forces in 1204–5, and in 1215 John had made him his justiciar or senior legal officer. Now Hubert led a vigorous defence of the castle, with a garrison that probably only numbered a few hundred men. The ensuing 'Great Siege', during which French troops caused the east tower of the north gate to collapse, only to be beaten off by the valiant garrison (see feature, page 25), lasted until 14 October 1216, when Louis lifted the siege.

Dover had been saved, but only just. Four days later John died suddenly. His nine-year-old son was proclaimed King Henry III, but half his kingdom was in the hands of the rebels and French invaders. The truce lasted until May 1217 when Louis besieged Dover again, but again it held out, and by this time the rebel cause was flagging. Hubert's valiant defence of Dover had been a key factor in the Angevin dynasty's survival.

Above: A reconstruction of
the castle at its height, in the
mid 13th century
Below: Detail from the
tomb effigy of Henry III in
Westminster Abbey

THE REIGN OF HENRY III
Completion of the Castle

After King John's death in October 1216, Hubert de Burgh became one of the leading members of the regency government for the young King Henry (r.1216–72). He was constable of Dover and Windsor castles and the Tower of London, and he supervised major works at all three, which applied the lessons learned in the sieges. The whole scutage of Kent (payments in lieu of castle-guard) was assigned to rebuilding Dover, as well as the royal revenues of Kent, Norfolk and Suffolk – Hubert was the sheriff of all three counties.

Between 1217 and 1221 the huge sum of £4,865 was spent on the castle. It is impossible to know how much of this went on building works, as the castle had a permanent garrison which cost about £1,000 a year to maintain. In these years Hubert strengthened (and possibly completed) the outer curtain walls, blocked up the old main gatehouse, built some remarkable underground works in the area, and added the new Constable's Gate to replace the old gate (see page 26). In the 1220s between 200 and 300 'fossatores', or ditch-diggers, were employed under Ralph of Popeshal, probably working on the outer banks and ditches, though they may have raised the great earth bank around the church.

In 1227 Henry III, aged 19, declared himself of full age, and rewarded Hubert for his loyal service by making him Earl of Kent. Five years later, however, Hubert fell from grace when the king became suspicious of his power: he was stripped of his offices and briefly imprisoned. Although restored to favour before his death in 1243, he never recovered his former authority and wealth.

Dover was now one of the largest and most strategically important castles in England. Work had continued inside the castle, with a new granary (1227) and windmill (1234–5). Henry III was one of the great royal builders of the Middle Ages: he added fine new royal lodgings to many royal residences, including Dover, where a new great hall – Arthur's Hall – and royal chambers were added to Henry II's inner bailey in 1236–44 (see page 11). In his reign the castle was effectively completed, and after about 1256 there were no more major alterations or additions to its defences until the 18th century.

The Siege of 1265

The 1260s saw a protracted political crisis in England, with Henry III's government challenged by the baronial opposition led by Simon de Montfort, Earl of Leicester. In July 1263 de Montfort captured Dover Castle, and in May 1264, after the king's defeat at the Battle of Lewes, the future Edward I was briefly held prisoner here.

In June 1265 de Montfort's wife, Eleanor, took possession of the castle, but on 4 August the rebels were defeated at the Battle of Evesham, when de Montfort was killed. At Dover, the widowed countess hired 29 archers, and prepared to hold out. Events took a dramatic turn when 14 royalist knights whom she had imprisoned managed to free themselves with the aid of some of the garrison; the royalists then barricaded themselves in the great tower. Prince Edward brought forces from London to besiege the castle. Eleanor and her garrison, under pressure both from outside and from within, surrendered to Edward, who was her nephew; she was treated courteously and allowed to go into exile. The events had, at least, demonstrated the strength of Henry II's great tower.

After this crisis, Henry III appointed Stephen of Penchester as constable of the castle and Lord Warden of the Cinque Ports. Stephen is thought to have been the illegitimate son of Peter, Count of Savoy, and was a member of the important Savoyard faction at court associated with Henry's French wife, Eleanor of Provence. His arms were those of Savoy, a white cross on a red ground: they appear in the first line of the Dering Roll, which he is thought to have commissioned (see page 36). Stephen's long constableship, lasting until his death in 1299, seems to have been a period of stability and consolidation at the castle. He probably compiled the castle's statutes, and set up the Court of Castle Gate to enforce them.

Above: A supposed portrait of Eleanor de Montfort, who led the defence of the castle in 1265, from a 13th-century genealogy of the Kings of England

Below: An illuminated letter from the 'Treaty of Dover Castle', the most important of the many surviving medieval documents that relate to the castle. The Treaty is now at Knole in Kent

The Castle Garrison

As one of the largest castles in the British Isles, Dover was continuously garrisoned throughout the Middle Ages. A late 14th-century book, known as the 'Treaty of Dover Castle', gives details of how eight baronies were set up, probably by Henry II, whose 'knights' fees' were dedicated to providing the castle with a permanent garrison.

In peacetime the garrison, which was headed by the constable, may have numbered about 25–50 men. The castle had numerous officers, including a clerk of the exchequer to manage the money, a seneschal and a marshal to command the garrison, a warrener to look after the rabbit warren, and at least three chaplains.

The Treaty, a remarkable compilaton of early documents about the castle, also includes a copy of the castle's statutes, which probably date from the 13th century. These set out the guidelines for how the watch should be kept, how the gates should be guarded, and how discipline should be maintained. They also make elaborate provision for the religious life of the garrison, which was centred on the church of St Mary, and the services to be held there.

Above: The fireplaces in the great tower are ornamented with Edward IV's personal badge, the 'rose en soleil' – the White Rose of York surrounded by the sun's rays

Right: Edward IV receiving the Burgundian ambassador in audience, from a late 15th-century manuscript

Below: Dover Castle is seen on the left in this painting, now at Hampton Court, of Henry VIII's embarkation for Calais to meet Francis I of France at the Field of the Cloth of Gold in 1520

THE CASTLE IN THE LATER MIDDLE AGES

Despite the frequency of French attacks on the coast in the 14th century, little seems to have been spent on the castle's maintenance in the later Middle Ages. Nevertheless, the post of constable and Lord Warden tended to be given to important men: Richard II gave it to his favourite, Sir Simon de Burley, with £300 a year to support himself and the castle officers on condition that he lived there, an indication of its strategic significance. Burley fell victim to the turbulent politics of the time, being impeached for treason by the king's enemies in the Merciless Parliament of 1388 and executed.

No major works were carried out until the reign of Edward IV (r.1461–83). There are no surviving records that document his work, but he seems to have modernized the great tower to serve as an occasional residence. Its windows were enlarged, given mullions, and probably glazed for the first time; chimneys were cut through the walls, and fine fireplaces were installed. This upgrading may have reflected Dover's position on the route to the Continent and the county of Flanders, which was ruled by the Dukes of Burgundy, Edward's most important foreign allies. We do not know, however, whether Edward ever saw the remodelled castle.

TUDOR DOVER

In the 16th century many of the Crown's fortresses began to fall into decay. Nonetheless, Dover remained a major garrisoned fortress because of its strategically important position and spacious accommodation. The Emperor Charles V stayed here in May 1520 (see page 15), and when Henry VIII (r.1509–47) crossed to France shortly afterwards for the diplomatic summit with Francis I of France known as the Field of the Cloth of Gold,

he embarked from Dover. Henry VIII visited Dover on several more occasions, especially during the difficult years after the Reformation, when England no longer had a major continental ally and was under renewed threat of invasion.

In December 1539 the great tower was refurbished again in anticipation of the arrival of Anne of Cleves, the German princess whom Henry had decided to marry as his fourth wife. The king's master-carpenter, James Needham, supervised alterations, including the installation of an iron crown and weathervane on top of the building. In the event Anne landed elsewhere, and Henry did not visit.

In these years Henry VIII had to address England's security. He rebuilt the royal fleet and constructed a remarkable new series of defences along the south coast, including nearby Deal and Walmer castles. The defence of Dover harbour was also addressed in 1539–40. Archcliffe Fort was built on the south-western flank of the harbour, and a gun battery called Moat's Bulwark was built at the foot of the castle cliff, covering the harbour from the north-east. Little seems to have been done to the castle itself, although a small gun battery from this period survives in the western moat just short of the cliff edge. A report of 1548 lists nine cannon apparently mounted near the cliff edge to direct fire down into the bay.

Elizabeth I visited the castle in 1573 as a guest of the constable, Lord Cobham, but when she returned in 1582 to say farewell to one of her foreign suitors, François, Duke of Alençon, brother of Henri III of France, she stayed in the town. The castle's derelict state may have inspired the major round of repairs that followed, for William Lambarde observed that 'our gracious Queen Elizabeth hath been at great charge in repairing the castle'. The first detailed views of the castle, such as John Bereblock's survey of the inner bailey (see page 9), record its appearance at this date.

THE 17TH CENTURY

The early 17th century saw the last chapter in Dover's history as an occasional or at least potential royal residence. In 1625 the castle was briefly occupied by Henrietta Maria, the teenage French princess who came to England to marry Charles I. Her retinue do not seem to have been very impressed by the castle: her chamberlain, Count Leveneur de Tillières, described the castle as 'an old building in the antique manner, where the queen was rather badly housed, poorly accommodated, and her train treated with very little magnificence, considering the occasion'. This may have helped to prompt its next major refurbishment in 1625–6, which was ordered by George Villiers, 1st Duke of Buckingham, James I's notoriously brash favourite. Buckingham had been created Lord Admiral of England as well as constable of Dover Castle and Lord Warden of the Cinque Ports, the first time all these offices had been combined, and he seems to have intended to remodel Dover as a headquarters for this new naval role.

Above: A 16th-century view of Dover from the sea, by Antonis van den Wyngaerde. At this date the harbour still lay to the west of the town

Below: Henrietta Maria, Queen Consort of Charles I, painted by Cornelius Janssens van Ceulen. Her entourage were unimpressed by the poor accommodation at the castle in 1625, and the great tower was never again used as a royal residence

Buckingham's most dramatic alteration was the addition of a 'greate Rusticke Dore', 23ft (7m) high and 13 ft (4m) wide, flanked by rusticated pilasters, as a grand new entrance at the foot of the steps to the great tower (this was demolished in 1746). The tower's interior, meanwhile, was completely redecorated with panelling and barrel-vaulted plaster ceilings, some of them painted by the Serjeant Painter John de Critz. Some of the other buildings were also renovated or rebuilt: the building with round-arched windows opposite the entrance to the great tower is the major survival from this period.

When the Civil War broke out in 1642 the town of Dover declared for Parliament, but the garrison of 20 remained loyal to Charles I. On the night of 21 August 1642, however, a daring merchant called Drake and 11 armed companions scaled the cliffs, surprised the garrison, and took the castle for Parliament with hardly a shot fired.

Dover escaped the slighting or deliberate destruction that was meted out to many medieval castles after the Civil War. A Parliamentarian garrison under Sir Algernon Sidney was manning the castle when a Royalist uprising broke out in Kent after the execution of Charles I in 1649; the rebels surrounded the castle, but scattered before Parliamentarian forces coming to the castle's relief.

Right: A view of Dover in 1746–7, by Richard Wilson
Below: *George Villiers, 1st Duke of Buckingham, who refurbished the castle in the 1620s while he was its constable and Lord Warden of the Cinque Ports, painted by Sir Peter Paul Rubens in 1625. The equestrian portrait for which this was the sketch was destroyed by fire in 1948*

The later 17th century was a period of neglect and picturesque decay. In June 1661 the garrison consisted of the Lord Warden, a 'gentleman gunner' and 17 gunners, probably concentrated down the cliff at Moat's Bulwark. Some time in the late 17th century the great tower was stripped and adapted to house French prisoners of war, a period commemorated in the many fine prisoner carvings around the building (see opposite).

DOVER TRANSFORMED
The Georgian Castle

The early 18th century saw the castle at its historic nadir. In 1708 it even lost its titular function as official residence of the Lord Warden of the Cinque Ports, when Lionel, 1st Duke of Dorset, holder of that office from 1707 until 1727, secured the use of Walmer Castle instead.

The castle's revival began during the War of the Austrian Succession (1740–48), when England faced a threat of French invasion in support of the

to adapt the curtain walls, starting with the northern stretch from Avranches Tower to the Norfolk Towers: the wall was reduced in height and a massive earth rampart built behind it. Bell Battery and Four Gun Battery were built higher up between the inner bailey and the Pencester Tower, to carry cannon that could cover the same stretch of wall. St John's Tower in the moat beyond the Norfolk Towers had its parapets modified for riflemen.

The Castle during the Napoleonic Wars

During the Revolutionary and Napoleonic Wars with France between 1793 and 1815, the threat of invasion was never greater. Dover was the most obvious target, with the French army camped just over the Strait at Boulogne. Prime Minister William Pitt's wartime government responded by spending about £500,000 on the town's defences, of which about £80,000 was spent on the castle.

The Napoleonic Wars are the second most important period for the development of Dover's defences, and Dover is one of the best places to see and understand Georgian military design in Britain. From 1792 to 1809 Lieutenant-Colonel (later Brigadier-General) William Twiss, one of the best military engineers of the age, was in charge of the works at Dover, with day-to-day supervision

Above: Moat's Bulwark at the foot of the castle cliff, from a view of the castle in 1801 by Francis Jukes

Below: One of the prisoner carvings, dated 1704, in the great tower

second Jacobite uprising of 1745. Any foreign army landing in England would need to capture a secure harbour to supply itself, and the most obvious target was Dover: so the defence of the harbour once again became a priority. The castle needed a larger garrison and better artillery defences, so the former medieval palace buildings in the inner bailey were remodelled as barracks in about 1745–6: they survive as some of the earliest purpose-built barracks in England. Further barracks were built at Moat's Bulwark and Archcliffe Fort, although these do not survive.

In 1756 the Seven Years War broke out, and England faced a renewed threat of invasion. The military engineer John Desmaretz, who was constructing defensive lines around the Royal Dockyard at Chatham, visited Dover to advise. More barrack space was needed, so the great tower was adapted for this purpose. Desmaretz also upgraded the castle's defences to improve their ability to withstand artillery attack. He began

Prisoner Carvings

By the first decade of the 18th century the great tower was being used as a prison, housing prisoners of war taken during the War of Spanish Succession (1702–14), in which England and her continental allies defeated Louis XIV's France. The carvings are concentrated mostly in three areas: in the first lobby of the forebuilding; around the entrance to the king's hall on the

second floor; and around the doors of the first-floor rooms. They are generally similar in form, one per stone, and the vast majority are simple signatures, many of which remain legible. Most of the names are

French, although a few are Flemish or Spanish, and not all the prisoners were soldiers or sailors: 'Francois de Mesnie marchant de Cherbourg mis prisoner le 23 juillet 1710' was a merchant.

from Captain William Ford. Twiss built new barracks, some as free-standing buildings, some in casemates, and some, when pressure on space within the castle became acute, in a remarkable complex of tunnels excavated beneath the castle. At the same time the castle's defences were overhauled to fit them for defence against artillery.

The rest of the town's defences were also being addressed, with major improvements to Archcliffe Fort down by the harbour, and to the Western Heights on the opposite side of the Dour valley, where nearly £230,000 was spent between 1804 and 1815. Twiss continued the work already begun on the Western Heights by Sir Thomas Hyde Page in the 1780s on the main Citadel at the south-west end and a large detached fort, Drop Redoubt, at the north-east end. These were linked by a line of defences on the northern side of the hill, and barrack space was provided, some of it in casemates, with room for a garrison of 1,500. Twiss's most famous work was the cylindrical shaft known as the Grand Shaft, cut through the chalk 8m in diameter and 42m deep, in which he built one masonry cylinder inside another to house three superimposed spiral staircases. Using these, soldiers could get from their barracks at the top down to Archcliffe Fort and the harbour in a matter of minutes. Over the next century, the castle and the Western Heights

were always considered jointly as the twin guardians of Dover and its harbour.

VICTORIAN DOVER

When peace was made with France in 1815, Dover's vast garrison was swiftly stood down. For over 30 years the castle stagnated, as in the early 18th century, with a very small establishment. From the 1850s, however, a major round of renovation and improvements to the defences took place, comparable in scale and scope to the late Georgian works. This time the perceived threat of invasion was from Napoleon III of France and his 'Second Empire'.

The mid-century works had three main aims: to defend Dover harbour and command the approaches to it with gunfire; to defend Dover and its harbour from a possible landward attack; and to make the castle fit to house a larger garrison. Admiralty Pier on the western side of the harbour was begun in 1847, the first stage in the building of a fully enclosed harbour which was only completed in 1907. The revolution in gunnery in the mid 19th century produced much more powerful guns, and the castle was provided with new batteries, all facing out to sea. On the Western Heights, which had been left unfinished on the return of peace in 1815, the Citadel was completed: further magazines, bastions and

Above: The Grand Shaft on the Western Heights, built by William Twiss, enabled soldiers to make a rapid descent from their barracks to the harbour

Right: The Western Heights. The Citadel, Drop Redoubt and other parts of the defences are in the care of English Heritage, and remain one of the most remarkable set-pieces of Georgian and Victorian military engineering in Britain

A Drop Redoubt
B Grand Shaft Barracks
C Citadel
D Western outworks

Left: In the 1890s the second floor of the great tower was furnished with displays of historic arms and armour. They were removed after the Second World War, when it was realized that the tower's damp conditions threatened their long-term wellbeing
Below: Louis Blériot landing at Dover after his pioneering flight over the Strait of Dover in July 1909

caponiers were added to it and other areas; a new main northern entrance was created; and a huge western extension was added to its defences. On completion, the Western Heights was probably the largest fortified enclosure in the British Isles.

There was little more that could be done to adapt the castle's medieval walls to meet the new threat. Instead a new fortress, Fort Burgoyne, was built to the north in about 1860–65, to cover the northern approaches to Dover. The town now had defences on a comparable scale to the rings of forts that surrounded the great naval bases at Plymouth, Portsmouth and Chatham.

Within the castle, new barracks were added, the most prominent being Salvin's Officers' New Barracks (see page 31). The restoration of the church as the garrison church (page 6) and construction of the Regimental Institute building (page 28) are testimony to the Victorian concern for the moral improvement of the soldiery.

THE CASTLE IN THE 20TH CENTURY

The 1890s saw the first indications that the castle might be valued for its historic interest. In about 1890 the top floor of the great tower was furnished with displays of armour and opened to the public; in 1898 the *pharos* was roofed; and in 1904 the church, *pharos* and Colton's Gate were

handed into the care of the Ancient Monuments Branch of the Ministry of Works, the predecessor of English Heritage.

Louis Blériot's flight across the Channel in 1909 (see below) presaged new threats to Britain, and during the First World War the Royal Flying Corps used Langdon Cliff, just north of the castle, as their

Louis Blériot

On 25 July 1909 the French aviator Louis Blériot made the first powered flight across the Channel. Setting off from Calais, he crash-landed on the hillside north-east of Dover Castle, guided to the ground by a friend waving a large French tricolor. The Louis Blériot Memorial – a stone silhouette of his aircraft set into the turf – marks the spot where he landed.

Above: Communications equipment in the reconstructed coastal artillery operations room on Casemate level

Right: The castle seen from the north-west in late evening light

departure point to join the British Expeditionary Force in France. Throughout the First World War Dover harbour was one of the main links in the chain supplying Britain's armies in Europe.

During the Second World War Dover was again on the front line, but against attack from the air as well as the sea. The harbour remained one of the key bases from which the Navy controlled the Channel, while pylons were erected on Langdon Cliff to support a link in the nation's new radar defences. Deep under the castle and safe from aerial bombardment, the Napoleonic tunnels developed a new role as a naval headquarters. It was from these tunnels that the Dunkirk evacuation was planned in May–June 1940, and the defence of this most vulnerable part of the English coast was led; gun batteries from North Foreland in north Kent to Hastings in Sussex were controlled from here. Air attacks on this stretch of coast become so frequent that it earned the nickname Hellfire Corner. Later in the war the original tunnels, known as Casemate level, were extended, and two new levels were excavated to provide more space for a secure combined headquarters as well as a hospital (see page 34).

After the Second World War, the castle emptied again. It was finally losing its military significance: the coastal batteries were becoming obsolete in the age of the guided missile, and the castle's last gun batteries were scrapped in 1956. The first battalion of the Queen's Own Cameron Highlanders was the last regular military unit to be quartered here, leaving in October 1958. Since then, the occupation of Constable's Gate by the deputy constable has been the castle's last link with the armed forces. In 1963 the rest of the above-ground castle was handed to the Ministry of Works for preservation as an Ancient Monument.

The castle retained one last secret use. After the Cuban Missile Crisis of 1962, which brought the world to the brink of nuclear war, the tunnels were renovated and equipped to serve as one of 12 Regional Seats of Government in the event of nuclear war, on the assumption that an attack would destroy London and central government. They retained this ghostly virtual life, packed with unused supplies, until the early 1980s. The castle has adapted to every generation of warfare from William the Conqueror to the Cold War, a record of continuity that is without parallel in Britain.